T0418369

# The Tip

## Consultants

**Ashley Bishop, Ed.D.**

**Sue Bishop, M.E.D.**

## Publishing Credits

Dona Herweck Rice, *Editor-in-Chief*

Robin Erickson, *Production Director*

Lee Aucoin, *Creative Director*

Tim J. Bradley, *Illustrator Manager*

Janelle Bell-Martin, *Illustrator*

Sharon Coan, *Project Manager*

Jamey Acosta, *Editor*

Rachelle Cracchiolo, M.A.Ed., *Publisher*

## Teacher Created Materials

5301 Oceanus Drive

Huntington Beach, CA 92649-1030

http://www.tcmpub.com

**ISBN 978-1-4333-2931-9**

**dip**

I see a dip.

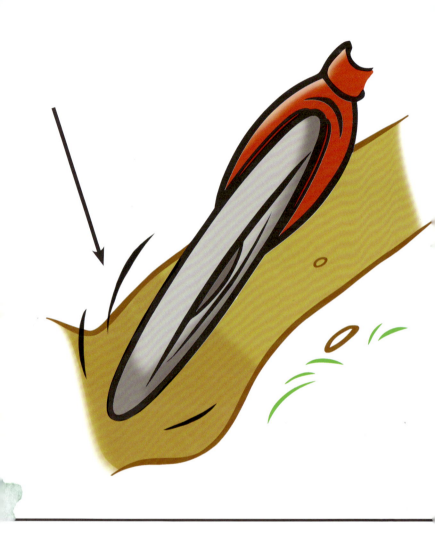

**tip**

I tip.

rip

I see a rip.

# hip

I see my hip.

# I need a sip!

# Glossary

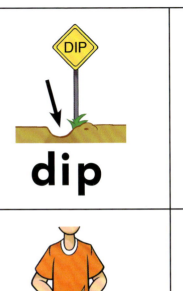

**dip**

**hip**

**rip**

**sip**

**tip**

## Sight Words

I   see

a   my

need

# Extension Activities

Read the story together with your child. Use the discussion questions before, during, and after your reading to deepen your child's understanding of the story and the rime (word family) that is introduced.

The activities provide fun ideas for continuing the conversation about the story and the vocabulary that is introduced. They will help your child make personal connections to the story and use the vocabulary to describe prior experiences.

## Discussion Questions

- Where is the dip in the story? Why does the boy tip?
- What are some ways that clothes rip?
- Why do we take sips? When was the last time you had a sip of something?
- Do you know how to ride a bicycle? Have you ever tipped over on your bike?

## Activities at Home

- Have your child find examples of *-ip* words at home. They may see the tip of a pencil or a rip in a piece of clothing. They may spot a family member taking a sip of something to drink. As your child finds *-ip* words, review the letters of the rime and the sound of the word.
- Work with your child to write sentences with the *-ip* words. Make each sentence relatable to your child's everyday life.